"If you think things look good now," she says, "just wait 'til you see everything else I've got in mind."

She's wildly excited
   about the day because
it's a brand new one,
   and new things
always make her feel more
   than just a little hopeful.

She has a gift
for seeing beauty,
like a bright and
sudden balloon,
floating along
beside her.

There is something radiant
about her. No denying it. She
used to think it was something
to do with what she was wearing
that day, but then she realized
it was her spirit shining.

After all the ups and downs out in the world, she came home to herself one day and realized she was perfect company.

Her faith in
what the future
brings is
greater than
any uncertainty.
It's clear that something
splendid is coming.

She leaned into her
deepest potential,
and all good things
leaned back.